D1156706

A SHARD OF SILENCE

SELECTED POEMS OF

Amy Lowell

A SHARD OF SILENCE

EDITED BY G. R. RUIHLEY

NEW YORK : TWAYNE PUBLISHERS, INC.

PRINTED IN THE UNITED STATES OF AMERICA

Designed by Sidney Solomon

TO

BEATRICE RUIHLEY

For Her Part in This

—G. R.

Contents

Acknowledgments

The editor is deeply grateful to Mr. Harvey Bundy and Mr. G. d'Andelot Belin, Trustees of the Amy Lowell Estate, for their kind permission to reprint Miss Lowell's work. Thanks are also due to my friends Bruce Fawcett and Professor Herbert Barrows, who have given me invaluable assistance and advice. I am, furthermore, indebted to Jerome Stone and John Ciardi, whose unselfish efforts in Amy Lowell's behalf have made possible the publication of this volume.

Introduction

IN A MEMORABLE STUDY of Amy Lowell printed in 1939, one of our leading critics voiced a judgment of the poet that has been widely endorsed. Comprehending little of her character, the critic wrote that Miss Lowell could not win "permanence as a poet" since she failed as a person: "how could she have attained it? She had many pleasures, few ecstasies; she wept because of little griefs, never touched by immedicable woes." The poetry lacks meaning, he insists, because understanding was sacrificed for brilliance, while the poet's variety of forms could not mask her "central poverty." If we add Clement Wood's complaint that Amy Lowell did not understand grammar, and Jean Catel's reference to a "diluted personality," insulated from life by inherited wealth, we have most of what we should know about criticism of the poet. Yet we are no closer to an understanding of Amy Lowell, nor have we arrived at a just estimate of her worth.

Both the forms of Amy Lowell's life and the record of her poetry suggest a nature shaken by inner stress. While still in early youth, Miss Lowell was afflicted with an illness that distended her body. The medicine of the day and prescribed diets failed her. In time she developed a bulk of flesh that caused her embarrassment as well as physical pain. She was to find herself disbarred from a normal experience of life. In writing about the poet, Elizabeth Sergeant refers to "the sense of a lost paradise." It was Amy Lowell's sharp awareness of promise given and withheld that vitalized her emotion. In the presence of a consuming lack, common experiences took on new meaning: the sight of withered leaves along a path, a spray of mignonette, a garden statue of Hermes of reproachful beauty. She saw these with feeling sufficient to transmute them into noble structures of sound:

Vengeful god of smooth, imperishable loveliness,
You are more savage than the goat-legged Pan,
Than the crocodile of carven yew-wood.
Fisherman of men's eyes,
You catch them on a three-pronged spear:
Your youth, your manhood,
The reticence of your ever-lasting revelation.
I too am become a cunning eye
Seeking you past your time-gnawed surface,
Seeking you back to hyacinths upon a dropping hill,
Where legend drowses in a glaze of sea.

Yours are the eyes of a bull and a panther,
For all that they are chiselled out and the sockets empty.
You—perfectly imperfect . . .
Borrowing the eyes of fruits and flowers—
And mine also, cold, impossible god,
So that I stare back at myself
And see myself with loathing.

We should not discredit Amy Lowell because her meanings have eluded us. Miss Lowell gave herself fully to her art, to the extent that she could anticipate an early death as the price of her purposes. Much of her printed verse is unworthy of her talent, being little more than adumbrations of the distinction found in other poems. While her narratives may express her love of color and movement, they are often empty and labored. In all probability the inferior verse did "spring from the will." The poet believed that she must produce a massive volume of work if she was to endure. These facts constrict the fullest enjoyment of her poetry. Coupled with the reaction to her eccentric mode of life, they account for the general distrust of her value. But a fair appraisal does not stress failings. What matters to us is Amy Lowell's substantial achievement, embodied in some fifty fresh and lucent poems.

In a perceptive study of Amy Lowell, included in his *Essays in Appreciation,* John Livingston Lowes quoted one of her lyrics and commented: "If those eight lines of 'Venus

Transiens' were the only fragment left of an unknown poet, we should recognize that the craftsmanship which wrought their cool, controlled, and shining beauty was unique." This beauty suggested to him "the clarity of radiant air and the pure lines of a pattern cut in polished stone." We would agree that the poet's chill purity of line was an essential value of her work. Notable even in certain early poems and sustained until we reach her last somber verse, this quality remains the touchstone of her art:

Over the housetops,
Above the rotating chimney-pots,
I have seen a shiver of amethyst,
And blue and cinnamon have flickered
A moment,
At the far end of a dusty street.

Through sheeted rain
Has come a lustre of crimson,
And I have watched moonbeams
Hushed by a film of palest green.

Its appeal is the beauty of the inviolable: seamless, final, complete. If it is sometimes remote, it can also be rich and suggestive. In these slight lines the poet catches up the melancholy of autumn and the muffled grief of passing years:

In the cloud-grey mornings
I heard the herons flying;
And when I came into my garden,
My silken outer-garment
Trailed over withered leaves.
A dried leaf crumbles at a touch,
But I have seen many Autumns
With herons blowing like smoke
Across the sky.

Amy Lowell read some poems of the Imagist school in 1912, when this poetry was first printed in America. In 1913 she was in England making the acquaintance of Ezra Pound and the others of his group. With that contact the writer of tepid, academic verse emerged as a creative artist. In the Imagist insistence on spontaneous language, direct statement, and, above all, the pictorial qualities of poetry, Amy Lowell found her innate mode of expression. The shifting poetic vision was fixed, pin-pointed in words, and its effect on the observer galvanized in free rhythms. The later poems, "Lilacs," "The Congressional Library," "In Excelsis," full-bodied and luxuriant as the movements of a symphony, were the extension of that technique.

Poetry, whether it be Hebrew, Latin, or American, transmits its message through pictures. To disparage a poet for being imagistic is to deny the nature of the art. Amy Lowell's abounding imagery was one of the signal resources of a fecund talent. Flashing through her verse like a bright-tinted bird or refined to the moving symbols of "Nuit Blanche," it infuses her poems with their most expressive element:

I will not think of sunset, I crave the dawn.
With its rose-red light on the wings of a swan,
And a queen pacing slowly through the Parthenon,
Her dress a stare of purple between pillars of stone.

Edwin Markham has said that Amy Lowell's verse was too often concerned with "the outer aspect of things": forms held up naked to the eyes of the reader. In fact, much of the verse is drawn from the sun-filled vistas of the poet's garden. Does this narrow the importance of the poems or, perhaps, suggest their value? To a degree remarkable in the history of poetry, Amy Lowell was conscious of the emotional import of material forms: a line of foliage across a sunken basin, lilacs flung up against the side of a hill; and she succeeded in defining their relation to our life:

Red foxgloves against a yellow wall streaked
with plum-colored shadows;
A lady with a blue and red sunshade;

The slow dash of waves upon a parapet.
That is all.
Non-existent—immortal—
As solid as the center of a ring of fine gold.

The brilliant pictorialism that produced poems such as "Lilacs" has not been surpassed and is significant for the development of all poetry. Such faint praise as that which has damned Amy Lowell has focused on this quality of her art. Yet it was the poet herself, writing in *A Critical Fable,* who disdained an art of surface effects and pointed to the "impassioned" heart. The gesture expressed only the insensitivity of the critics. Since her first poem, celebrating Eleonora Duse, and written "with infinite agitation," the poet had plucked at the theme of her inner life. That it was a tortured life and that in consequence her ultimate development was remarkable gives the poetry of Amy Lowell its peculiar meaning and expressiveness.

In her first volume, *A Dome of Many Colored Glass,* she wrote:

. . . overshadowing all is still the curse
That never shall I be fulfilled by love!
Along the parching highroad of the world
No other soul shall bear mine company . . .
So I behold my visions on the ground
No longer radiant, an ignoble heap
Of broken, dusty glass. And so, unlit
Even by hope or faith, my dragging steps
Force me forever through the passing days.

This was to be a recurring theme of her poetry: a feminine nature, sensitive to the recreative forces of life, reaching for the fulfillment that could not be hers. She saw that experience finds its goal in self-knowledge and the completion of love. The sharp pain that surged through her from the hollowness of her life found its expression in memorable verse.

She asked in a poem: "And in December what birds sing!" Yet facing the winter of her life, she found substance for poetry luminous with meaning. To a degree everyone shares Amy Lowell's incompleteness and the longing for wider satisfactions that always dance beyond our grasp. In voicing her desire, the poet touched something fundamental in human experience. She speaks for everyone who senses an emotional lack in his life, who feels that he has not been permitted to realize his inner nature, who yearns to exchange dull routine for those adventures of the body and spirit through which a man may come to some knowledge of himself and of the world.

I would anything
Rather than this cold paper;
With outside, the quiet sun on the sides of burgeoning branches,
And inside, only my books.

The poems that spring from this theme: "Fool O' The Moon," "The Green Parakeet," "Free Fantasia on Japanese Themes" etc., are among Amy Lowell's most expressive work.

The search for roots that might hold her to life began early for Amy Lowell. It came with her first awareness that she must live alone, outside the quieting circle of family concerns. The poet inherited a large fortune and the mansion of Sevenels from her father, Augustus. This smoothed her path. But the heavy splendor of Sevenels would be a reproach to a sterile life. The daughter of the proud race sought an answer in a literary career. She found a personal solution in her friend, Ada Russell.

Amy Lowell first met Mrs. Russell, a widowed actress, at a luncheon club in 1912. They found that they shared many interests. After a trip together in England, Mrs. Russell came to live at Sevenels as the poet's assistant and companion. The pronounced affinity between them ripened into an extraordinary love. Safe in this warm garment, Amy Lowell could face the pain and disillusionments of her life.

It was the sight of Mrs. Russell seated in the garden or reading in the corner of a room that touched Amy Lowell's life with joy:

I cannot see your face.
When I think of you,
It is your hands which I see.
Your hands
Sewing,
Holding a book,
Resting for a moment on the sill of a window.
My eyes keep always the sight of your hands,
But my heart holds the sound of your voice,
And the soft brightness which is your soul.

The rich chambers of feeling newly opened to her softened and deepened her poetry. From the whispered contentment of "Penumbra" to the rapture of "In Excelsis," her poems sang of her love.

"Appuldercombe Park" written in Amy Lowell's later years begins with the refrain: "I am a woman sick for passion." "In a Time of Dearth" pictures the poet straining towards a mirage, but a sandstorm comes, "Suffocating me and making me struggle for air." In another poem we read:

Night lies beside me
Chaste and cold as a sharp sword.
It and I alone.

Friendship might light the way, but it could not answer the poet's dilemma. The blight of a misshapen body was irrevocable. There was no path to those ranges of pristine emotion she had sought—had sought too long. The defeat pushed out; encircled her. In *A Critical Fable* she wrote of herself: "The future's her goose and I dare say she'll wing it." Had she not been convinced by a carping criticism that her poetry was insubstantial, little more than an arresting experiment? She speaks of distrust of her work in a touching letter to Sara Teasdale. And the persistent ill-health, the spells of blindness, the too-heavy body supported by a cane took their toll. She says that she is "tired and afraid."

It was into this frame of life that Eleonora Duse stepped in 1923. The Italian actress had returned to America for a last tour, but the triumph she achieved here ended suddenly in death. Though Amy Lowell longed to help the artist during the difficult months of her tour, she did not succeed in easing the rigors of Duse's life.

Unknown to Madame Duse in Italy, the link between herself and Amy Lowell had been a focal point of the poet's life. In 1902 Duse had appeared in Boston in plays by d'Annunzio. Although Miss Lowell was already 28 at this time, the vision granted her at one of these performances was her awakening as a poet: "The effect was something tremendous. What really happened was that it revealed me to myself." The first poem was written the same evening; and a short time later when she met Madame Duse, the actress became Miss Lowell's life-long artistic ideal.

In 1923 this was already far in the past, and one may ponder the motives for Duse's return. Eleonora Duse at sixty-three was physically worn: "emaciated, white-haired, and frail." Although financially distressed, she had refused a pension from Mussolini. Upon arrival in New York, Duse herself expressed the wish to escape the troubled atmosphere of Europe. The traveling companion of the actress had written Amy Lowell from England. Learning of Duse's needs, Amy Lowell arranged to provide for them on the long tour.

In Boston after her performances Madame Duse visited her friend at Sevenels. Twenty-one years had passed since the vision that changed the immature woman into a poet. S. Foster Damon writes: "Surely Miss Lowell tried to tell her something of this; but of their conversation only one sentence remains: Duse's 'The past is dead; the future alone lives.' " Confronting Duse and facing the "wreckage of life,"

Amy Lowell wrote her most expressive poem, "Eleonora Duse."

In exalted tones she rejects material values and announces the function of the artist in clarifying and extending the confines of human life. True, the years had been cruel, but they could not dim Duse's radiant beauty:

. . . all disguise
Time can achieve is but to add a stress,
A finer fineness, as though some caress
Touched you a moment to a strange surprise.

Amy Lowell was greatly moved by the meeting. In the bond she felt with Duse her life seemed to be renewed. She says that we may rise above the forces of change and destruction; that out of suffering can come strength; and that, by holding tight to those with whom we share the darkness, the avenues of experience broaden, and, with deepened knowledge, the terrors of the world disappear.

G.R.

1

Patterns

I walk down the garden paths,
And all the daffodils
Are blowing, and the bright blue squills.
I walk down the patterned garden paths
In my stiff, brocaded gown.
With my powdered hair and jewelled fan,
I too am a rare
Pattern, as I wander down
The garden paths.

My dress is richly figured,
And the train
Makes a pink and silver stain
On the gravel, and the thrift
Of the borders.
Just a plate of current fashion
Tripping by in high-heeled, ribboned shoes.
Not a softness anywhere about me,
Only whalebone and brocade.
And I sink on a seat in the shade
Of a lime tree. For my passion
Wars against the stiff brocade.
The daffodils and squills
Flutter in the breeze
As they please.
And I weep;
For the lime tree is in blossom
And one small flower has dropped upon my bosom.

And the plashing of waterdrops
In the marble fountain
Comes down the garden paths.
The dripping never stops.
Underneath my stiffened gown
Is the softness of a woman bathing in a marble basin,
A basin in the midst of hedges grown
So thick, she cannot see her lover hiding,
But she guesses he is near,
And the sliding of the water
Seems the stroking of a dear
Hand upon her.
What is Summer in a fine brocaded gown!
I should like to see it lying in a heap upon the ground.
All the pink and silver crumpled up on the ground.

I would be the pink and silver as I ran along the paths,
And he would stumble after,
Bewildered by my laughter.
I should see the sun flashing from his sword-hilt
    and the buckles on his shoes.
I would choose
To lead him in a maze along the patterned paths,
A bright and laughing maze for my heavy-booted lover.
Till he caught me in the shade,
And the buttons of his waistcoat bruised my body as he
    clasped me,
Aching, melting, unafraid.
With the shadows of the leaves and the sundrops,
And the plopping of the waterdrops,
All about us in the open afternoon—
I am very like to swoon
With the weight of this brocade,
For the sun sifts through the shade.

Underneath the fallen blossom
In my bosom,
Is a letter I have hid.
It was brought to me this morning by a rider from the duke.
"Madam, we regret to inform you that Lord Hartwell
Died in action Thursday se'nnight."
As I read it in the white, morning sunlight,
The letters squirmed like snakes.
"Any answer, Madam," said my footman.
"No," I told him.
"See that the messenger takes some refreshment.
No, no answer."
And I walked into the garden,
Up and down the patterned paths,
In my stiff, correct brocade.
The blue and yellow flowers stood up proudly in the sun,
Each one.
I stood upright too,
Held rigid to the pattern
By the stiffness of my gown.
Up and down I walked.
Up and down.

In a month he would have been my husband.
In a month, here, underneath this lime,
We would have broken the pattern;
He for me, and I for him,
He as Colonel, I as Lady,
On this shady seat.
He had a whim
That sunlight carried blessing.
And I answered, "It shall be as you have said."
Now he is dead.

In Summer and in Winter I shall walk
Up and down
The patterned garden paths
In my stiff, brocaded gown.
The squills and daffodils
Will give place to pillared roses, and to asters and to snow.
I shall go
Up and down,
In my gown.
Gorgeously arrayed,
Boned and stayed.
And the softness of my body will be guarded from embrace
By each button, hook, and lace.
For the man who should loose me is dead,
Fighting with the Duke in Flanders,
In a pattern called a war.
Christ! What are patterns for?

2

Ada Russell

Song For A Viola D'Amore

The lady of my choice is bright
As a clematis at the touch of night,
As a white clematis with a purple heart
When twilight cuts earth and sun apart.
Through the dusking garden I hear her voice
As a smooth, sweet, wandering, windy noise,
And I see her stand as a ghost may do
In answer to a rendezvous
Long sought with agony and prayer.
So watching her, I see her there.

I sit beneath a quiet tree
And watch her everlastingly.
The garden may or may not be
Before my eyes, I cannot see.
But darkness drifting up and down
Divides to let her silken gown
Gleam there beside the clematis.
How marvelously white it is!
Five white blossoms and she are there
Like candles in a fluttering air
Escaping from a tower stair.

Be still you cursed, rattling leaf,
This is no time to think of grief.

The night is soft, and fire-flies
Are very casual, gay, and wise,
And they have made a tiny glee
Just where the clematis and she
Are standing. Since the sky is clear,
Do they suppose that, once a year,
The moon and five white stars appear
Walking the earth; that, so attended,
Diana came and condescended
To hold speech with Endymion
Before she came at last alone.

The lady of my choice is bright
As a clematis at the fall of night.
Her voice is honeysuckle sweet,
Her presence spreads an April heat
Before the going of her feet.
She is of perfectness complete.
The lady whom my heart perceives
As a clematis above its leaves,
As a purple-hearted clematis.
And what is lovelier than that is?

Venus Transiens

Tell me,
Was Venus more beautiful
Than you are,
When she topped
The crinkled waves,
Drifting shoreward
On her plaited shell?
Was Botticelli's vision
Fairer than mine;
And were the painted rosebuds
He tossed his lady,
Of better worth
Than the words I blow about you
To cover your too great loveliness
As with a gauze
Of misted silver?

For me,
You stand poised
In the blue and buoyant air,
Cinctured by bright winds,
Treading the sunlight.
And the waves which precede you
Ripple and stir
The sands at my feet.

Madonna Of The Evening Flowers

All day long I have been working,
Now I am tired.
I call: "Where are you?"
But there is only the oak tree rustling in the wind.
The house is very quiet,
The sun shines in on your books,
On your scissors and thimble just put down,
But you are not there.
Suddenly I am lonely:
Where are you?
I go about searching.

Then I see you,
Standing under a spire of pale blue larkspur,
With a basket of roses on your arm.
You are cool, like silver,
And you smile.
I think the Canterbury bells are playing little tunes.

You tell me that the peonies need spraying,
That the columbines have overrun all bounds,
That the pyrus japonica should be cut back and rounded.
You tell me these things.
But I look at you, heart of silver,
White heart-flame of polished silver,
Burning beneath the blue steeples of the larkspur,
And I long to kneel instantly at your feet,
While all about us peal the loud, sweet *Te Deums* of the
    Canterbury bells.

A Sprig Of Rosemary

I cannot see your face.
When I think of you,
It is your hands which I see.
Your hands
Sewing,
Holding a book,
Resting for a moment on the sill of a window.
My eyes keep always the sight of your hands,
But my heart holds the sound of your voice,
And the soft brightness which is your soul.

The Garden By Moonlight

A black cat among roses,
Phlox, lilac-misted under a first-quarter moon,
The sweet smells of heliotrope and night-scented stock.
The garden is very still,
It is dazed with moonlight,
Contented with perfume,
Dreaming the opium dreams of its folded poppies.
Firefly lights open and vanish
High as the tip buds of the golden glow
Low as the sweet alyssum flowers at my feet.
Moon-shimmer on leaves and trellises,
Moon-spikes shafting through the snow-ball bush.
Only the little faces of the ladies' delight are alert
and staring,
Only the cat, padding between the roses,
Shakes a branch and breaks the chequered pattern
As water is broken by the falling of a leaf.
Then you come,
And you are quiet like the garden,
And white like the alyssum flowers,
And beautiful as the silent sparks of the fireflies.
Ah, Beloved, do you see those orange lilies?
They knew my mother,
But who belonging to me will they know
When I am gone.

The Giver Of Stars

Hold your soul open for my welcoming.
Let the quiet of your spirit bathe me
With its clear and rippled coolness,
That, loose-limbed and weary, I find rest,
Outstretched upon your peace, as on a bed of ivory.

Let the flickering flame of your soul play all about me,
That into my limbs may come the keenness of fire,
The life and joy of tongues of flame,
And, going out from you, tightly strung and in tune,
I may rouse the blear-eyed world,
And pour into it the beauty which you have begotten.

Thorn Piece

Cliffs,
Cliffs,
And a twisted sea
Beating under a freezing moon.
Why should I,
Sitting peaceful and warm,
Cut my heart on so sharp a tune?

Liquid lapping of seething fire
Eating the heart of an old beech tree.
Crack of icicles under the eaves,
Dog-wind whining eerily.

The oaks are red, and the asters flame,
And the sun is warm on bark and stones.
There's a Hunter's Moon abroad tonight—
The twigs are snapping like brittle bones.

You carry a lantern of rose-green glass,
Your dress is red as a Cardinal's cloak.
I kneel at the trace of your feet on the grass,
But when I would sing you a song, I choke.

Choke for the fragile careless years
We have scattered so easily from our hands.
They flutter like leaves through an Autumn sun,
One by one, one by one.

I have lived in a place,
I shall die in a place,
I have no craving for distant lands.
But a place is nothing, not even space,
Unless at its heart a figure stands

Swinging a rose-green lantern for me.
I fear the fall of a rose-green gate,
And the cry of a cliff-driven, haunted sea,
And the crackle of ice while I wait—wait!

Your face is flowers and singing sun,
Your hands are the cool of waters falling.
If the rose-green bars should drop between
Would you know that I was calling?

For the stars I see in that sky are black.
The kind earth holds me and laughs in my ear.
I have nothing to do with the planet's track,
I only want you, my Dear.

Beyond is a glaze, but here is fire,
And love to comfort, and speech to bind,
And the common things of morning and evening,
And the light of your lantern I always find.

One or the other—then let it be me,
For I fear the whirl of the cliff-wrung sea,
And the biting night. You smile at my fears,
But the years—years—
Like leaves falling.

A Decade

When you came, you were like red wine and honey,
And the taste of you burnt my mouth with its sweetness.
Now you are like morning bread,
Smooth and pleasant.
I hardly taste you at all for I know your savor,
But I am completely nourished.

Penumbra

As I sit here in the quiet Summer night,
Suddenly, from the distant road, there comes
The grind and rush of an electric car.
And, from still farther off,
An engine puffs sharply,
Followed by the drawn-out shunting scrape of a
freight train.
These are the sounds that men make
In the long business of living.
They will always make such sounds,
Years after I am dead and cannot hear them.

Sitting here in the Summer night,
I think of my death.
What will it be like for you then?
You will see my chair
With its bright chintz covering
Standing in the afternoon sunshine,
As now.
You will see my narrow table
At which I have written so many hours.
My dogs will push their noses into your hand,
And ask—ask—
Clinging to you with puzzled eyes.

The old house will still be here,
The old house which has known me since the beginning.
The walls which have watched me while I played:
Soldiers, marbles, paper-dolls,
Which have protected me and my books.

The front-door will gaze down among the old trees
Where, as a child, I hunted ghosts and Indians;
It will look out on the wide gravel sweep
Where I rolled my hoop,
And at the rhododendron bushes
Where I caught black-spotted butterflies.

The old house will guard you,
As I have done.
Its walls and rooms will hold you,
And I shall whisper my thoughts and fancies
As always,
From the pages of my books.

You will sit here, some quiet Summer night,
Listening to the puffing trains,
But you will not be lonely,
For these things are a part of me.
And my love will go on speaking to you
Through the chairs, and the tables, and the pictures,
As it does now through my voice,
And the quick, necessary touch of my hand.

3

The Captured Goddess

Over the housetops,
Above the rotating chimney-pots,
I have seen a shiver of amethyst,
And blue and cinnamon have flickered
A moment,
At the far end of a dusty street.

Through sheeted rain
Has come a lustre of crimson,
And I have watched moonbeams
Hushed by a film of palest green.

It was her wings,
Goddess!
Who stepped over the clouds,
And laid her rainbow feathers
Aslant on the currents of the air.

I followed her for long,
With gazing eyes and stumbling feet.
I cared not where she led me,
My eyes were full of colors:
Saffrons, rubies, the yellows of beryls,
And the indigo-blue of quartz;
Flights of rose, layers of chrysoprase,
Points of orange, spirals of vermilion,
The spotted gold of tiger-lily petals,
The loud pink of bursting hydrangeas.
I followed,
And watched for the flashing of her wings.

In the city I found her,
The narrow-streeted city.
In the market-place I came upon her,
Bound and trembling.
Her fluted wings were fastened to her sides with cords,
She was naked and cold,
For that day the wind blew
Without sunshine.

Men chaffered for her,
They bargained in silver and gold,
In copper, in wheat,
And called their bids across the market-place.

The Goddess wept.

Hiding my face I fled,
And the grey wind hissed behind me,
Along the narrow streets.

Irony

An arid daylight shines along the beach
Dried to a grey monotony of tone,
And stranded jelly-fish melt soft upon
The sun-baked pebbles, far beyond their reach
Sparkles a wet, reviving sea. Here bleach
The skeletons of fishes, every bone
Polished and stark, like traceries of stone,
The joints and knuckles hardened each to each.
And they are dead while waiting for the sea,
The moon-pursuing sea, to come again.
Their hearts are blown away on the hot breeze.
Only the shells and stones can wait to be
Washed bright. For living things, who suffer pain,
May not endure till time can bring them ease.

Convalescence

From out the dragging vastness of the sea,
Wave-fettered, bound in sinuous, sea-weed strands,
He toils toward the rounding beach, and stands
One moment, white and dripping, silently,
Cut like a cameo in lazuli,
Then falls, betrayed by shifting shells, and lands
Prone in the jeering water, and his hands
Clutch for support where no support can be.
So up, and down, and forward, inch by inch,
He gains upon the shore, where poppies glow
And sandflies dance their little lives away.
The sucking waves retard, and tighter clinch
The weeds about him, but the land-winds blow,
And in the sky there blooms the sun of May.

Meeting-House Hill

I must be mad, or very tired,
When the curve of a blue bay beyond a railroad track
Is shrill and sweet to me like the sudden springing of a tune,
And the sight of a white church above thin trees in a
city square
Amazes my eyes as though it were the Parthenon.
Clear, reticent, superbly final,
With the pillars of its portico refined to a cautious elegance,
It dominates the weak trees,
And the shot of its spire
Is cool and candid,
Rising into an unresisting sky.
Strange meeting-house
Pausing a moment upon a squalid hill-top.
I watch the spire sweeping the sky,
I am dizzy with the movement of the sky,
I might be watching a mast
With its royals set full
Straining before a two-reef breeze.
I might be sighting a tea-clipper,
Tacking into the blue bay,
Just back from Canton
With her hold full of green and blue porcelain
And a Chinese coolie leaning over the rail
Gazing at the white spire
With dull, sea-spent eyes.

Music

The neighbor sits in his window and plays the flute.
From my bed I can hear him,
And the round notes flutter and tap about the room,
And hit against each other,
Blurring to unexpected chords.
It is very beautiful,
With the little flute-notes all about me,
In the darkness.

In the daytime,
The neighbor eats bread and onions with one hand
And copies music with the other.
He is fat and has a bald head,
So I do not look at him,
But run quickly past his window.
There is always the sky to look at,
Or the water in the well!

But when night comes and he plays his flute,
I think of him as a young man,
With gold seals hanging from his watch,
And a blue coat with silver buttons.
As I lie in my bed
The flute-notes push against my ears and lips,
And I go to sleep, dreaming.

A Lady

You are beautiful and faded
Like an old opera tune
Played upon a harpsichord;
Or like the sun-flooded silks
Of an eighteenth-century boudoir.
In your eyes
Smoulder the fallen roses of outlived minutes,
And the perfume of your soul
Is vague and suffusing,
With the pungence of sealed spice-jars.
Your half-tones delight me,
And I grow mad with gazing
At your blent colors.

My vigor is a new-minted penny,
Which I cast at your feet.
Gather it up from the dust,
That its sparkle may amuse you.

The Broken Fountain

Oblong, its jutted ends rounding into circles,
The old sunken basin lies with its flat, marble lip
An inch below the terrace tiles.
Over the stagnant water
Slide reflections:
The blue-green of coned yews;
The purple and red of trailing fuchsias
Dripping out of marble urns;
Bright squares of sky
Ribbed by the wake of a swimming beetle.
Through the blue-bronze water
Wavers the pale uncertainty of a shadow.
An arm flashes through the reflections,
A breast is outlined with leaves.
Outstretched in the quiet water
The statue of a goddess slumbers.
But when Autumn comes
The beech leaves cover her with a golden counterpane.

Sultry

To those who can see them, there are eyes,
Leopard eyes of marigolds crouching above red earth,
Bulging eyes of fruits and rubies in the heavily-hanging
    trees,
Broken eyes of queasy cupids staring from the gloom
    of myrtles.
I came here for solitude
And I am plucked at by a host of eyes.

A peacock spreads his tail on the balustrade
And every eye is a mood of green malice,
A challenge and a fear.
A hornet flashes above geraniums,
Spying upon me in a trick of cunning.
And Hermes,
Hermes the implacable,
Points at me with a fractured arm.

Vengeful god of smooth, imperishable loveliness,
You are more savage than the goat-legged Pan,
Than the crocodile of carven yew-wood.
Fisherman of men's eyes,
You catch them on a three-pronged spear:
Your youth, your manhood,
The reticence of your everlasting revelation.
I too am become a cunning eye
Seeking you past your time-gnawed surface,
Seeking you back to hyacinths upon a dropping hill,
Where legend drowses in a glaze of sea.

Yours are the eyes of a bull and a panther,
For all that they are chiselled out and the sockets empty.
You—perfectly imperfect,
Clothed in a garden,
In innumerable gardens,
Borrowing the eyes of fruits and flowers—
And mine also, cold, impossible god,
So that I stare back at myself
And see myself with loathing.

A quince-tree flings a crooked shadow—
My shadow, tortured out of semblance,
Bewildered in quince boughs.
His shadow is clear as a scissored silhouette.
Heat twinkles and the eyes glare.
And I, of the mingled shadow,
I glare
And see nothing.

Haunted

See! He trails his toes
Through the long streaks of moonlight,
And the nails of his fingers glitter:
They claw and flash among the tree-tops.
His lips suck at my open window,
And his breath creeps about my body
And lies in pools under my knees.
I can see his mouth sway and wobble,
Sticking itself against the window-jambs,
But the moonlight is bright on the floor,
Without a shadow.
Hark! A hare is strangling in the forest,
And the wind tears a shutter from the wall.

Chinoiseries

Reflections

When I looked into your eyes,
I saw a garden
With peonies, and tinkling pagodas,
And round-arched bridges
Over still lakes.
A woman sat beside the water
In a rain-blue silken garment.
She reached through the water
To pluck the crimson peonies
Beneath the surface,
But as she grasped the stems,
They jarred and broke into white-green ripples;
And as she drew out her hand,
The water-drops dripping from it
Stained her rain-blue dress like tears.

Falling Snow

The snow whispers about me,
And my wooden clogs
Leave holes behind me in the snow.
But no one will pass this way
Seeking my footsteps,
And when the temple bell rings again
They will be covered and gone.

Hoar-Frost

In the cloud-grey mornings
I heard the herons flying;
And when I came into my garden,
My silken outer-garment
Trailed over withered leaves.
A dried leaf crumbles at a touch,
But I have seen many Autumns
With herons blowing like smoke
Across the sky.

Little Ivory Figures Pulled With String

Is it the tinkling of mandolins which disturbs you?
Or the dropping of bitter-orange petals among the
coffee-cups?
Or the slow creeping of the moonlight between the
olive-trees?
Drop! drop! the rain
Upon the thin plates of my heart.

String your blood to chord with this music,
Stir your heels upon the cobbles to the rhythm of a
dance-tune.
They have slim thighs and arms of silver;
The moon washes away their garments;
They make a pattern of fleeing feet in the branch shadows,
And the green grapes knotted about them
Burst as they press against one another.
The rain knocks upon the plates of my heart,
They are crumpled with its beating.

Would you drink only from your brains, Old Man?
See, the moonlight has reached your knees,
It falls upon your head in an accolade of silver.
Rise up on the music,
Fling against the moon-drifts in a whorl of young light
bodies:
Leaping grape-clusters,
Vine leaves tearing from a grey wall.

You shall run, laughing, in a braid of women,
And weave flowers with the frosty spines of thorns.
Why do you gaze into your glass,
And jar the spoons with your finger-tapping?
  The rain is rigid on the plates of my heart.
  The murmur of it is loud—loud.

Fool O' The Moon

The silver-slippered moon
Treads the blue tiles of the sky,
And I
See her dressed in golden roses,
With a single breast uncovered,
The carnation tip of it
Urgent for a lover's lip.
So she dances to a stately
Beat, with poses most sedately
Taken, yet there lies
Something wanton in her gestures,
And there is surprise of coquetry
In the falling of her vestures.
Why?

Out of old mythology,
With a pulse of gourds and sheepskins,
Banging bronze and metal thunders,
There is she,
Wonderfullest of earth's wonders.
As for me,
Head thrown back and arms spread wide
Like a zany crucified,
I stand, watching, waiting, gazing,
All of me spent in amazing,
Longing for her wheat-white thighs,
Thirsting for her emerald fire,
My desire
Pounding dully from my eyes.
And my hands
Clutch and cuddle the vast air
Seeking her where she's most fair.

There,
On the cool blue tiles of heaven,
She is dancing cooly, coldly,
Footsteps trace a braid of seven,
And her gauzy garments fleet
Round her like a glittering sleet.
Suddenly she flings them boldly
In a streaming bannerall
Out behind,
And I see all.
God! I'm blind!

And a goodly company
Of men are we,
Lovers she has chosen,
Laughing-stocks and finger-posts
To the wise, a troupe of ghosts
Swelled by every century.

Mad, and blind, and burnt, and frozen,
Standing on a hilly slope
At bright midnight,
And our hope
Is in vain, or is it not?
Legend knows the very spot
Where the moon once made her bed.
But the pathway as it led
Over rock-brows to that valley
Is an alley choked and dead.
One by one our fates deceive us,
One of hundreds will be shown
Ferny uplands whose great bosses
Of tall granite hide the mosses
Where our Lady's lying prone,

All her stars withdrawn, alone.
So she chooses to receive us,
Out of hundreds, only one.

Such a vale of moss and heather
Spreads about us, hither—thither.
Hush!
Shall I tell what befell
Once behind that bush.
When the rattling pods at noon
Made a music in September.
Shall I say what I remember—
While the long, sea-grasses croon,
And the sea-spray on the sand
Chips the silence from the land?
Hush, then, let me say it soon.
I have lain with Mistress Moon.

4

In Excelsis

You—you—
Your shadow is sunlight on a plate of silver;
Your footsteps, the seeding-place of lilies;
Your hands moving, a chime of bells across a windless air.

The movement of your hands is the long, golden running
of light from a rising sun;
It is the hopping of birds upon a garden path.

As the perfume of jonquils, you come forth in the morning.
Young horses are not more sudden than your thoughts,
Your words are bees about a pear-tree,
Your fancies are the gold-and-black striped wasps buzzing
among red apples.
I drink your lips,
I eat the whiteness of your hands and feet.
My mouth is open,
As a new jar I am empty and open.
Like white water are you who fill the cup of my mouth,
Like a brook of water thronged with lilies.

You are frozen as the clouds,
You are far and sweet as the high clouds.
I dare reach to you,
I dare touch the rim of your brightness.
I leap beyond the winds,
I cry and shout,
For my throat is keen as a sword
Sharpened on a hone of ivory.
My throat sings the joy of my eyes,
The rushing gladness of my love.

How has the rainbow fallen upon my heart?
How have I snared the seas to lie in my fingers
And caught the sky to be a cover for my head?
How have you come to dwell with me,
Compassing me with the four circles of your mystic
lightness,
So that I say "Glory! Glory!" and bow before you
As to a shrine?

Do I tease myself that morning is morning and a day after?
Do I think the air a condescension,
The earth a politeness,
Heaven a boon deserving thanks?
So you—air—earth—heaven—
I do not thank you,
I take you,
I live.
And those things which I say in consequence
Are rubies mortised in a gate of stone.

White Currants

Shall I give you white currants?
I do not know why, but I have a sudden fancy for this fruit.
At the moment, the idea of them cherishes my senses,
And they seem more desirable than flawless emeralds.
Since I am, in fact, empty-handed,
I might have chosen gems out of India,
But I choose white currants.
Is it because the raucous wind is hurtling round the
 house-corners?
I see it with curled lips and striped fangs, gaunt with a
 hunting energy,
Come to snout, and nibble, and kill the little crocus roots.
Shall we call it white currants?
You may consider it as a symbol if you please.
You may find them tart, or sweet, or merely agreeable
 in color,
So long as you accept them,
And me.

Merely Statement

You sent me a sprig of mignonette,
Cool-colored, quiet, and it was wet
With green sea-spray, and the salt and the sweet
Mingled to a fragrance weary and discreet
As a harp played softly in a great room at sunset.

You said: "My sober mignonette
Will brighten your room and you will not forget."

But I have pressed your flower and laid it away
In a letter, tied with a ribbon knot.
I have not forgot.
But there is a passion-flower in my vase
Standing above a close-cleared space
In the midst of a jumble of papers and books.
The passion-flower holds my eyes,
And the light-under-light of its blue and purple dyes
Is a hot surprise.
How then can I keep my looks
From the passion-flower leaning sharply over the books?
When one has seen
The difficult magnificence of a queen
On one's table,
Is one able
To observe any color in a mignonette?
I will not think of sunset, I crave the dawn,
With its rose-red light on the wings of a swan,
And a queen pacing slowly through the Parthenon,
Her dress a stair of purple between pillars of stone.

White and Green

Hey! My daffodil-crowned,
Slim and without sandals!
As the sudden spurt of flame upon darkness
So my eyeballs are startled with you,
Supple-limbed youth among the fruit-trees,
Light runner through tasseled orchards.
You are an almond flower unsheathed
Leaping and flickering between the budded branches.

Anticipation

I have been temperate always,
But I am like to be very drunk
With your coming.
There have been times
I feared to walk down the street
Lest I should reel with the wine of you,
And jerk against my neighbors
As they go by.
I am parched now, and my tongue is horrible in my mouth,
But my brain is noisy
With the clash and gurgle of filling wine-cups.

The Taxi

When I go away from you
The world beats dead
Like a slackened drum.
I call out for you against the jutted stars
And shout into the ridges of the wind.
Streets coming fast,
One after the other,
Wedge you away from me,
And the lamps of the city prick my eyes
So that I can no longer see your face.
Why should I leave you,
To wound myself upon the sharp edges of the night?

Opal

You are ice and fire,
The touch of you burns my hands like snow.
You are cold and flame.
You are the crimson of amaryllis,
The silver of moon-touched magnolias.
When I am with you,
My heart is a frozen pond
Gleaming with agitated torches.

Paradox

You are an amethyst to me,
Beating dark slabs of purple
Against quiet smoothnesses of heliotrope,
Sending the wine-color of torches
Rattling up against an avalanche of pale windy leaves.

You enter my heart as twilight
Seeping softly among the ghosts of beeches
In a glade where the last light cleaves for an instant upon
the swung lash of a waterfall.
You oversweep me with the spendid flashing of your
darkness,
And my flowers are tinted with the light of your thin grey
moon.

An amethyst garden you are to me,
And in your sands I write my poems,
And plant my heart for you in deathless yew trees
That their leaves may shield you from the falling snow.

Open your purple palaces for my entertainment,
Welcome my feet upon your polished floors,
And keep in your brazier always
One red hot coal;
For I come at the times which suit me,
Morning or evening,
And I am cold when I come down the long alleys to you.
Clang the doors against the multitude who would follow me.
Is not this my chamber where I would sleep?

Patience

Be patient with you?
When the stooping sky
Leans down upon the hills
And tenderly, as one who soothing stills
An anguish, gathers earth to lie
Embraced and girdled. Do the sun-filled men
Feel patience then?

Be patient with you?
When the snow-girt earth
Cracks to let through a spurt
Of sudden green, and from the muddy dirt
A snowdrop leaps, how mark its worth
To eyes frost-hardened, and do weary men
Feel patience then?

Be patient with you?
When pain's iron bars
Their rivets tighten, stern
To bend and break their victims; as they turn,
Hopeless, there stand the purple jars
Of night to spill oblivion. Do these men
Feel patience then?

Be patient with you?
You! My sun and moon!
My basketful of flowers!
My money-bag of shining dreams! My hours,
Windless and still, of afternoon!
You are my world and I your citizen.
What meaning can have patience then?

In Answer To A Request

You ask me for a sonnet. Ah, my dear,
Can clocks tick back to yesterday at noon?
Can cracked and fallen leaves recall last June
And leap up on the boughs, now stiff and sere?
For your sake, I would go and seek the year,
Faded beyond the purple ranks of dune,
Blown sands of drifted hours, which the moon
Streaks with a ghostly finger, and her sneer
Pulls at my lengthening shadow. Yes, 'tis that!
My shadow stretches forward, and the ground
Is dark in front because the light's behind.
It is grotesque, with such a funny hat,
In watching it and walking I have found
More than enough to occupy my mind.
I cannot turn, the light would make me blind.

5

The Congressional Library

The earth is a colored thing.
See the red clays, and the umbers and salt greys of the
mountains;
See the clustered and wandering greens of plains and
hillsides,
The leaf-greens, bush-greens, water-plant and snow-greens
Of gardens and forests.
See the reds of flowers—hibiscus, poppy, geranium;
The rose-red of little flowers—may-flowers, primroses;
The harlequin shades of sweet-peas, orchids, pansies;
The madders, saffrons, chromes, of still waters,
The silver and star-blues, the wine-blues of seas and oceans.
Observe the stars at nighttime, name the color of them;
Count and recount the hues of clouds at sunset and at dawn.
And the colors of the races of men—
What are they?
And what are we?
We, the people without a race,
Without a language;
Of all races, and of none;
Of all tongues, and one imposed;
Of all traditions and all pasts,
With no tradition and no past.
A patchwork and an altar-piece,
Vague as sea-mist,
Myriad as forest-trees,
Living into a present,
Building a future.
Our color is the vari-colored world.
No colors clash,
All clash and change,

And, in changing, new colors come and go and dominate
and remain,
And no one shall say which remain,
Since those that have vanished return,
And those no man has seen take the light and are.

Where else in all America are we so symbolized
As in this hall?
White columns polished like glass,
A dome and a dome,
A balcony and a balcony,
Stairs and the balustrades to them,
Yellow marble and red slabs of it,
All mounting, spearing, flying into color.
Color round the dome and up to it,
Color curving, kite-flying, to the second dome,
Light, dropping, pitching down upon the color,
Arrow-falling upon the glass-bright pillars,
Mingled colors spinning into a shape of white pillars,
Fusing, cooling, into balanced shafts of shrill and
interthronging light.
This is America,
This vast, confused beauty,
This staring, restless speed of loveliness,
Mighty, overwhelming, crude, of all forms,
Making grandeur out of profusion,
Afraid of no incongruities,
Sublime in its audacity,
Bizarre breaker of moulds,
Laughing with strength,
Charging down on the past,
Glorious and conquering,
Destroyer, builder,
Invincible pith and marrow of the world,

An old world remaking,
Whirling into the no-world of all-colored light.

But behind the vari-colored hall?
The entrails, the belly,
The blood-run veins, the heart and viscera,
What of these?
Only at night do they speak,
Only at night do the voices rouse themselves and speak.
There are words in the veins of this creature,
There are still notes singing in its breast:
Silent voices, whispering what it shall speak,
Frozen music beating upon its pulses.
These are the voices of the furious dead who never die,
Furious with love, and life, unquenchable,
Dictating their creeds across the vapors of time.
This is the music of the Trumpeters of the Almighty
Weeping for a lost estate,
Sounding to a new birth which is tomorrow.
Hark! This hurricane of music has no end,
The speech of these voices has neither end nor beginning;
They are inter-riven as the colors of the sky
Over the graveyards of ten thousand generations.

When we are as Nineveh, our white columns thrown and
scattered,
Our dome of colors striped with the crawling of insects,
Spotted with the thrust of damp clay—
Our words, our music, who will build a dome to hive them?
In whose belly shall we come to life?
A new life,
Beyond submergence and destruction,
The implacable life of silent words,
Of tumultuous stillness of never-ceasing music,

Lost to being that so it may triumph
And become the blood and heat and urge
Of that hidden distance which forever whips and harries
the static present
Of mankind.

East, West, North, And South Of A Man

1

He rides a white horse,
  Mary Madonna,
Dappled as clouds are dappled,
  O Mary, Mary,
And the leather of his harness is the color of the sky.

On his head is a casque with an azure plume
Which none may observe with unswerving eyes.
  A proud gentleman, Mary Madonna.
A knight to fill the forest, riding it cross-wise,
  O Mary, Mary.
His hoof-prints dint the breech-mast,
His plume brushes the golden leaves.

No flute man this to sigh at a lady's elbow.
This is a trumpet fellow, proper for jousting or battle,
  Mary Madonna,
To hack an enemy to pieces, and scale his castle wall.
  O Mary, Mary,
A point for piercing, an edge for shearing, a weight for
    pounding, a voice for thundering,
And a fan-gleam light to shine down little alleys
Where twisted houses make a jest of day.

There are dead men in his hand,
  Mary Madonna,
And sighing women out beyond his thinking.
  O Mary, Mary,
He will not linger here or anywhere.

He will go about his business with an ineradicable
complaisance,
Leaving his dead to rot, his women to weep and regret,
his sons to wax into his likeness,
Never dreaming that the absurd lie he believes in
Is a gesture of Fate forcing him to the assumption of a
vast importance
Quite other than the blazoning of ceremonial banners
to wave above a tomb.

2

Hot with oranges and purples,
In a flowing robe of a marigold color,
He sweeps over September spaces.
Scheherezade, do you hear him,
And the clang of his scimitar knocking on the gates?
The tawny glitter of his turban,
Is it not dazzling—
With the saffron jewel set like a sunflower in the midst?
The brown of his face!
Aye, the brown like the heart of a sunflower.
Who are you to aspire beyond the petals,
To touch the golden burning beneath the marigold robe?
His sash is magnificence clasped by an emerald;
His scimitar is the young moon hanging before a sunset;
His voice is the sun in mid-heaven
Pouring on whirled ochre dahlias;
His fingers, the flight of Autumn wasps through a
honey-colored afternoon.
So, Scheherezade, he has passed the dragon fountains
And is walking up the marble stairway, stopping to caress
the peacocks.
He will lean above you, Scheherezade, like September
above an orchard of apples.

He will fill you with the sweetness of spice-fed flames.
Will you burn, Scheherezade, as flowers burn in September
sunlight?
Hush, then, for flame is silence,
And silent is the penetrating of the sun.

The dragon fountains splash in the courtyards,
And the peacocks spread their tails.
There are eyes in the tails of the peacocks,
But the palace windows are shuttered and barred.

3

Pipkins, pans, and pannikins,
China teapots, tin and pewter,
Baskets woven of green rushes.
Maudlin, Jennifer, and Prue,
What is lacking in your kitchens?
Are you needing skewers or thimbles,
Spools of cotton, knots of ribbon,
Or a picture for your pantry,
Or a rag-rug for the bed-side?
Plodding, plodding, through the dusty
Lanes between the hawthorn hedges,
My green wheels all white and dusty,
I as dusty as a miller,
White as any clown among them
Dancing on the London stages.
Here I have Grimaldi's latest,
Songs and ballads, sheets of posies
For your feet to ring-a-rosy.
Songs to make you sigh and shudder,
Songs to win you bright eye-glances,
Choruses, and glees, and catches.
Do your cupboards need refilling?

Take a peep into these hampers.
I have goods to loose your purse-strings:
Smocks, and shifts, and fine clocked stockings
Aprons of a dozen sizes,
Muslin dresses sprigged and patterned.
Can you look and not be buying?
Maudlin, Jennifer, and Prue,
Here are dainties for sweetheartings,
Tinsel crackers plumped with mottoes,
Twisted barley sticks and pear-drops.
Here are ear-rings, chains, and brooches,
Choose what gift you'll have him give you.
If the sweetheart days are over,
I have silver forks and bodkins,
Leather breeches, flannel bed-gowns,
Spectacles for eyes grown feeble,
Books to read with them and candles
To light up the page of evenings.
Toys, too, to delight the children,
Rocking horses, tops, and marbles,
Dolls with jointed arms, and flying
Kites, and hoops, and even the Royal
Game of Goose the world is playing.
When I camp out on a common,
Underneath an oak or linden,
And my horse crops at his supper,
Finding it along the hedge-rows,
Then I play at Goose with one hand
Taking sides against the other.
First my right hand holds the dice-cup,
Then my left, each has its counter.
'Tis a pastime never tires.
Coppers, coppers, for the pedlar.
Maudlin, Jennifer, and Prue,

Fare you well, I must be jogging.
Horse-bells tinkle at the lane-sides,
Green wheels growing whiter, whiter,
Lurching van of whims and whimsies
Vanishing into the distance.

4

Who would read on a ladder?
But who can read without a ladder?
Cheerful paradox to be resolved never.
Book by book, he steps up and off to all the four quarters
Of all the possible distances.
  Minerva have a care of him,
  For surely he has none for himself.
His eyes are dim with the plague of print,
But he believes them eagle-seeing.
His spectacles have grown to his nose,
But he is unaware of the fact since he never takes them off.
A little black cap on his head;
A rusty dressing-gown, with the quilts run together,
To keep out the cold;
A window out of which he never looks;
A chair from which he never rises.
But do you not know a wharf-side when you see it,
And are you not moved at watching the putting off of the
    caravels of dream?
Food gets into his mouth by accident
As though fish swam the seas to come there,
And cattle crowded the thoroughfares to reach his lips.
If there are intermediaries, he is unconscious of them,
As he is of everything but his cat,
Who shares his vigils
And has discovered the art of projecting herself into his
    visions.

He loves a thousand ladies, and foregathers with a thousand caravans.
Today is as remote as yesterday,
And he is avid of either with the intensity of a partaker of each;
He could hobnob as blithely with Julius Caesar as with King George or Samuel Gompers,
And his opinions on affairs of the moment are those of an eyewitness
Although he never sets foot out-of-doors.
Indeed, Minerva, you should watch the step of this gentleman,
For he runs so swiftly past events and monuments it seems incredible he should not trip.
The walls of forbidden cities fall before him;
He has but to tap a sheepskin to experience kingdoms,
And circumstance drips from his fingers like dust.
An habituated eye sees much through a pin-prick,
And are not his observations folio wide?
He eats the centuries
And lives a new life every twenty-four hours,
So lengthening his own to an incalculable figure.
If you think you see only an old man mouldering between four walls,
You are greatly mistaken.
Minerva over the door could tell you better
If her stone face would speak.
Talk to him and he will not hear you;
Write a book and he knows you better than you know yourself.
Draw the curtains, then, and bring in tea, with plenty of buttered scones.
Since neither the old gentleman nor Minerva will speak to us,
I think we had best ignore them and go on as we are.

The Vow

Tread softly, softly,
Scuffle no dust.
No common thoughts shall thrust
Upon this peaceful decay,
This mold and rust of yesterday.
This is an altar with its incense blown away
By the indifferent wind of a long, sad night;
These are the precincts of the dead who die
Unconquered. Haply
You who haunt this place
May deign some gesture of forgiveness
To those of our sundered race
Who come in all humility
Asking an alms of pardon.
Suffer us to feel an ease,
A benefice of love poured down on us from these
        magnolia-trees.
That, when we leave you, we shall know the bitter wound
Of our long mutual scourging healed at last and sound.

Through an iron gate, fantastically scrolled and garlanded,
Along a path, green with moss, between two rows of high
        magnolia-trees—
  How lightly the wind drips through the magnolias.
  How slightly the magnolias bend to the wind.
It stands, pushed back into a corner of the piazza,
A jouncing-board, with its paint scaled off,
A jouncing-board which creaks when you sit upon it.
  The wind rattles the stiff leaves of the magnolias;
  So may tinkling banjos drown the weeping of women.

When the Yankees came like a tide of locusts,
When blue uniforms blocked the ends of streets
And foolish, arrogant swords struck through the paintings of a hundred years.
From gold and ivory coasts come the winds that jingle in the tree-tops;
But the sigh of the wind in the unshaven grass, from whence is that?

Proud hearts who could not endure desecration,
Who almost loathed the sky because it was blue;
Vengeful spirits locked in young, arrogant bodies,
You cursed yourselves with a vow;
Never would you set foot again in Charleston streets,
Never leave your piazza till Carolina was rid of Yankees.
O smooth wind sliding in from the sea,
It is a matter of no moment to you what flag you are flapping.

Ocean tides, morning and evening, slipping past the sea-islands;
Tides slipping in through the harbor, shaking the palmetto posts,
Slipping out through the harbor;
Pendulum tides, counting themselves upon the sea-islands.

So they jounced, for health's sake,
To be well and able to rejoice when once again the city was free,
And the lost cause won, and the stars and bars afloat over Sumter.
The days which had roared to them called more softly,
The days whispered, the days were silent, they moved as imperceptibly as mist.

And the proud hearts went with the days, into the dusk of age, the darkness of death.
Slowly they were borne away through a Charleston they scarcely remembered.
The jouncing-board was pushed into a corner,
Only the magnolia-trees tossed a petal to it, now and again, if there happened to be a strong wind when the blooms were dropping.

Hush, go gently,
Do not move a pebble with your foot.
This is a moment of pause,
A moment to recollect the futility of cause.
A moment to bow the head
And greet the unconcerned dead,
Denying nothing of their indifference,
And then go hence
And forget them again,
Since lives are lived with living men.

In The Stadium

Marshall Joffre Reviewing The
Harvard Regiment, May 12, 1917

A little old man
Huddled up in a corner of a carriage,
Rapidly driven in front of throngs of people
With his hand held to a perpetual salute.
The people cheer,
But he has heard so much cheering.
On his breast is a row of decorations.
He feels his body recoil before attacks of pain.

They are all like this:
Napoleon,
Hannibal,
Great Caesar even,
But that he died out of time.
Sick old men,
Driving rapidly before a concourse of people,
Gay with decorations,
Crumpled with pain.

The drum-major lifts his silver-headed stick,
And the silver trumpets and tubas,
The great round drums,
Each with an H on them,
Crash out martial music.
Heavily rhythmed march music
For the stepping of a regiment.

Slant lines of rifles,
A twinkle of stepping,
The regiment comes.
The young regiment,
Boys in khaki
With slanted rifles.
The young bodies of boys
Bulwarked in front of us.
The white bodies of young men
Heaped like sandbags
Against the German guns.

This is war:
Boys flung into a breach
Like shoveled earth;
And old men,
Broken,
Driving rapidly before crowds of people
In a glitter of silly decorations.

Behind the boys
And the old men,
Life weeps,
And shreds her garments
To the blowing winds.

Folie De Minuit

No word, no word, O Lord God!
Hanging above the shivering pillars
Like thunder over a brazen city.

Pity? Is there pity?
Does pity pour from the multiform points
Of snow crystals?
If the throats of the organ pipes
Are numb with cold,
Can the boldest bellows' blast
Melt their now dumb hosannas?

No word, august and brooding God!
No shrivelled spectre of an aching tone
Can pierce those banners
Which hide your face, your hands,
Your feet at whose slight tread
Frore water curds to freckled sands
Seaweed encrusted.
The organ loft is draughty with faint voices
Weeping,
Which are not mine, nor would be.
I purposed anthems, copper-red and golden,
Thrusting to the hearts of Babylonian Kings,
Bowed down before Judea and its Highest,
That God of Hosts who screens himself with banners.
My finger-tips are cast in a shard of silence;
The wormy lips of these great, narrow tunnels, the pipes,
Are choked with silence;
The banners, the banners, are brittle with decay
And rusted out of color.

The candles gutter in their sconces,
Curling long welts of evil-smelling smoke about my head.
The organ's voice is dead,
Or is it mine?
The banners flap
Like palls upon a bier
On windy midnight burials
Where torches flare a glittering imposture
About the loneliness of violated sod
Gashed open for a grave.

Pity me, then,
Who cry with wingless psalms,
Spellbound in midnight and chill organ pipes.
Above my eyes the banners bleed
Their dripping dust-specks,
Proclaiming the gaunt glories of successful battles.
It would enchant me to see you afloat behind them,
Blown for a moment to an eye-catch.
But who are you to come for frozen Hallelujahs!

And yet I go on silently playing.

A Rhyme Out Of Motley

"I grasped a thread of silver; it cut me to the bone—
I reached for an apple; it was bleak as a stone—
I reached for a heart, and touched a raw blade—
And this was the bargain God had made
For a little gift of speech
Set a cubit higher than the common reach,
A debt running on until the fool is dead."

Carve a Pater Noster to put at his head
As a curse or a prayer,
And leave him there.

The Green Parakeet

"Three doors up from the end of the street
Hung a golden cage with a green parakeet."
His feet shambled in the dust of the road, and the little barberry bushes hung out red tongues and leered at him.
He shuffled on, down the road, bent as though it might be a load he was carrying, while tiers and tiers of poplars, birches, hemlocks, pines, peered to see who it might be who stumbled and flung the dust about,
And the grey grape-vines, in and out between the bushes, ran beside him and looked in his face.
But his pace never changed a whit for all their staring. He shuffled on at his long way-faring.

"Morning and night, to the green parakeet
She sang, and oh, her singing was sweet!"
The road dipped down to a marsh, and the meadow-larks sang as he passed them, but his ears rang with another singing so that he heard nothing.
"By the North Wind's whistle, he is blind!" said a moose-wood to an elder-bush.
"Hush," cried the grape-vines, "you do not catch his dust. It is the dust of something a long way off."

"Her kisses were a flower red;
I saw them on the bird's green head.
Her breasts were white as almond bean
And the parakeet nestled in between."
"Oh, gently, gently," sighed the sentimental vines, but the

long lines of trees behind them objected that he took a great while to go by.

"We are better employed," they declared, "contemplating the sky."

Then I knocked at the door and entered in
Like the orange flame of a hidden sin.
I stood before her and there were three—
The parakeet and I and she.
I tossed her arms apart and pressed
Myself upon her, breast to breast,
And the parakeet was my bidden guest.
I forced her lips till they caught on mine,
And poured myself down her throat like wine.
I mingled with her, part for part,
But the parakeet lay next her heart.
Oh, sweeter than her lips were sweet
Was my utter hate for that parakeet.
She fell from me like the withered shell
Of a cranberry, and it was well;
I stood on the other side of Hell.
Slowly, slowly, she raised her head,
But the parakeet fell down like lead
Upon the matting, still and dead.
Softly, softly, she gazed at me,
And I saw a thing which I dared not see.
"My love!" she said and the tones were sweet
As ever she used to the parakeet.
But I had made my flaming breast
A weapon to kill a bird on its nest—
A single flame for the bird and me,
And I was as smothered as he could be.
I stared at her from the farther side
Of Hell, no space is great beside

This space. I could not see her face
Across such vastitude of space,
And over it drowsed a darkened thing:
A monster parakeet's green wing.
The air was starred with parakeets.
I turned and rushed into the streets.
For days and days I wandered there,
For oh! My love was very fair!
Each night I watched her lean and stand,
With empty heart and empty hand,
While every passer-by she scanned.
But I beheld what was not meet
For all to see—a parakeet
Of gauzy substance which could cast
No slightest shadow where it passed,
Fluttering with indecent glee
Between my hungering love and me.
Ten months went by, and then one day
It struck my face and flew away.
Some odd obedience in my feet
Compelled me after, street by street,
And then along a country lane.
I had no power to turn again.
Next morning took me farther still,
My feet usurped the place of will.
And now I walk a weary road,
Bent double underneath the load
Of memory and second sight.
That bird is always on my right
And just ahead, I follow where
His body flickers through the air.
Sometimes it is as plain as print,
Sometimes no better than a hint
Of color where no leaves are green.

But I can see what I have seen.
How many years is that ago?
I notice night and morning flow
Each into each, the seasons run
Against the turning of the sun,
But more or fewer—'tis all one.
She may be dead, and I may be
A ghost myself, eternally
Dreaming the short, ironic bliss
Of one long, unrepeated kiss.

The man scuffed across a bridge and up a steep hill.
"Quietly, quietly," whispered the barberry-bushes,
And hid their scarlet tongues under the leaves.
"Weep, Tree-Brothers," said the grape-vines.
But the long lines of trees only rustled and played hide and seek with the peeping moon.
They were too tall to pay much heed to anything so small as an old man limping up a hill.

Preface To An Occasion

How witless to assail the carven halls
Of memory! To climb the high stone steps,
Picking a foothold through the crisp, dry leaves
Whirled in the corners, crunching under foot
Those scattered in the center, to clap at doors
With battered hauberk, till some seneschal,
Drowsy with age and oversleeping, creaks
Them open an inhospitable inch,
And, grumbling, lets himself be pushed aside
By a determined entrance! Where's the sense
Of striding by tarnished furniture from one
Mournful deserted chamber to another,
Seeking for roses in a vase of dust,
For tapestries where rusty armour hangs,
For blithe allurement under spider-spun
Ceilings corroded to a dripping ash?
What can you find here? A little powdered dust
To pinch up with your finger and your thumb
And fasten in a knotted handkerchief!
Look from the window, Friend, the sky is blue,
The leafless trees blow to a merry wind,
Your horse is tethered at the stairway's foot,
He twitches at the skipping of the leaves.
Pocket your handkerchief and ride away.
Was the trip worth while? I'll wager guinea gold
Within a week you'll wish you had not come,
And send your handkerchief knotted to the wash.
Life's the great cynic, and there's an end of that.

On Looking At A Copy Of Alice Meynell's Poems

GIVEN ME YEARS AGO BY A FRIEND

Upon this greying page you wrote
A whispered greeting, long ago.
Faint pencil-marks run to and fro
Scoring the lines I loved to quote.

A sea-shore of white-shoaling sand,
Blue creeks zigzagging through marsh-grasses,
Sand pipers, and a wind which passes
Cloudily silent up the land.

Upon the high edge of the sea
A great four-master sleeps; three hours
Her bowsprit has not cleared those flowers.
I read and look alternately.

It all comes back again, but dim
As pictures on a winking wall
Hidden save when the dark clouds fall
Or crack to show the moon's bright rim.

I well remember what I was,
And what I wanted. You, unwise
With sore unwisdom, had no eyes
For what was patently the cause.

So are we sport of others' blindness,
We who could see right well alone.
What were you made of—wood or stone?
Yet I remember you with kindness.

You gave this book to me to ease
The smart in me you could not heal.
Your gift a mirror—woe or weal.
We sat beneath the apple-trees.

And I remember how they rang,
These words, like bronze cathedral bells
Down ancient lawns, or citadels
Thundering with gongs where choirs sang.

Silent the sea, the earth, the sky,
And in my heart a silent weeping.
Who has not sown can know no reaping!
Bitter conclusion and no lie.

O heart that sorrows, heart that bleeds,
Heart that was never mine, your words
Were like the pecking Autumn birds
Stealing away my garnered seeds.

No future where there is no past!
O cherishing grief which laid me bare,
I wrapped you like a wintry air
About me. Poor enthusiast!

How strange that tumult, looking back.
The ink is pale, the letters fade.
The verses seem to be well made,
But I have lived the almanac.

And you are dead these drifted years,
How many I forget. And she
Who wrote the book, her tragedy
Long since dried up its scalding tears.

I read of her death yesterday,
Frail lady whom I never knew
And knew so well. Would I could strew
Her grave with pansies, blue and grey.

Would I could stand a little space
Under a blowing, brightening sky,
And watch the sad leaves fall and lie
Gently upon that lonely place.

So cried her heart, a feverish thing.
But clay is still, and clay is cold,
And I was young, and I am old,
And in December what birds sing!

Go, wistful book, go back again
Upon your shelf and gather dust.
I've seen the glitter through the rust
Of old, long years, I've known the pain.

I've recollected both of you,
But I shall recollect no more.
Between us I must shut the door.
The living have so much to do.

6

Lilacs

Lilacs,
False blue,
White,
Purple,
Color of lilac,
Your great puffs of flowers
Are everywhere in this my New England.
Among your heart-shaped leaves
Orange orioles hop like music-box birds and sing
Their little weak soft songs;
In the crooks of your branches
The bright eyes of song sparrows sitting on spotted eggs
Peer restlessly through the light and shadow
Of all Springs.
Lilacs in dooryards
Holding quiet conversations with an early moon;
Lilacs watching a deserted house
Settling sideways into the grass of an old road;
Lilacs, wind-beaten, staggering under a lopsided shock of
bloom
Above a cellar dug into a hill.
You are everywhere.
You were everywhere.
You tapped the window when the preacher preached his
sermon,
And ran along the road beside the boy going to school.
You stood by pasture-bars to give the cows good milking,
You persuaded the housewife that her dishpan was of silver
And her husband an image of pure gold.
You flaunted the fragrance of your blossoms
Through the wide doors of Custom Houses—

You, and sandal-wood, and tea,
Charging the noses of quill-driving clerks
When a ship was in from China.
You called to them: "Goose-quill men, goose-quill men,
May is a month for flitting."
Until they writhed on their high stools
And wrote poetry on their letter-sheets behind the
propped-up ledgers.
Paradoxical New England clerks,
Writing inventories in ledgers, reading the "Song of
Solomon" at night,
So many verses before bed-time,
Because it was the Bible.
The dead fed you
Amid the slant stones of graveyards.
Pale ghosts who planted you
Came in the night-time
And let their thin hair blow through your clustered stems.
You are of the green sea,
And of the stone hills which reach a long distance.
You are of elm-shaded streets with little shops where they
sell kites and marbles,
You are of great parks where everyone walks and nobody
is at home.
You cover the blind sides of greenhouses
And lean over the top to say a hurry-word through the glass
To your friends, the grapes, inside.

Lilacs,
False blue,
White,
Purple,
Color of lilac,
You have forgotten your Eastern origin,

The veiled women with eyes like panthers,
The swollen, aggressive turbans of jeweled Pashas.
Now you are a very decent flower,
A reticent flower,
A curiously clear-cut, candid flower,
Standing beside clean doorways,
Friendly to a house-cat and a pair of spectacles,
Making poetry out of a bit of moonlight
And a hundred or two sharp blossoms.

Maine knows you,
Has for years and years;
New Hampshire knows you,
And Massachusetts
And Vermont.
Cape Cod starts you along the beaches to Rhode Island;
Connecticut takes you from a river to the sea.
You are brighter than apples,
Sweeter than tulips,
You are the great flood of our souls
Bursting above the leaf-shapes of our hearts,
You are the smell of all Summers,
The love of wives and children,
The recollection of the gardens of little children,
You are State Houses and Charters
And the familiar treading of the foot to and fro on a road
    it knows.
May is lilac here in New England,
May is a thrush singing "Sun up!" on a tip-top ash tree,
May is white clouds behind pine trees
Puffed out and marching upon a blue sky.
May is a green as no other,
May is much sun through small leaves,
May is soft earth,

And apple-blossoms,
And windows open to a South wind.
May is a full light wind of lilac
From Canada to Narragansett Bay.

Lilacs,
False blue,
White,
Purple,
Color of lilac.
Heart-leaves of lilac all over New England,
Roots of lilac under all the soil of New England,
Lilac in me because I am New England,
Because my roots are in it,
Because my leaves are of it,
Because my flowers are for it,
Because it is my country
And I speak to it of itself
And sing of it with my own voice
Since certainly it is mine.

Purple Grackles

The grackles have come.
The smoothness of the morning is puckered with their
incessant chatter.
A sociable lot, these purple grackles,
Thousands of them strung across a long run of wind,
Thousands of them beating the air-ways with quick
wing-jerks,
Spinning down the currents of the South.
Every year they come,
My garden is a place of solace and recreation evidently,
For they always pass a day with me.
With high good nature they tell me what I do not want
to hear.
The grackles have come.

I am persuaded that grackles are birds;
But when they are settled in the trees,
I am inclined to declare them fruits
And the trees turned hybrid blackberry vines.
Blackness shining and bulging under leaves,
Does not that mean blackberries, I ask you?
Nonsense! The grackles have come.

Nonchalant highwaymen, pickpockets, second-story
burglars,
Stealing away my little hope of summer.
There is no stealthy robbing in this.
Who ever heard such a gabble of thieves' talk!
It seems they delight in unmasking my poor pretense.
Yes, now I see that the hydrangea blooms are rusty;
That the hearts of the golden glow are ripening to lustreless
seeds;

That the garden is dahlia-colored,
Flaming with its last over-hot hues;
That the sun is pale as a lemon too small to fill the
picking-ring.
I did not see this yesterday,
But today the grackles have come.

They drop out of the trees
And strut in companies over the lawn,
Tired of flying, no doubt;
A grand parade to limber legs and give wings a rest.
I should build a great fish-pond for them,
Since it is evident that a bird-bath, meant to accommodate
two goldfinches at most,
Is slight hospitality for these hordes.
Scarcely one can get in.
They all peck and scrabble so,
Crowding, pushing, chasing one another up the bank with
spread wings.
"Are we ducks, you, owner of such inadequate comforts,
That you offer us lily-tanks where one must swim or drown,
Not stand and splash like a gentleman?"

I feel the reproach keenly, seeing them perch on the edges
of the tanks, trying the depth with a chary foot,
And hardly able to get their wings under water in the
bird-bath.
But there are resources I had not considered,
If I am bravely ruled out of count.
What is that thudding against the eaves just beyond my
window?
What is that spray of water blowing past my face?
Two—three—grackles bathing in the gutter,
The gutter providentially choked with leaves.

I pray they think I put the leaves there on purpose;
I would be supposed thoughtful and welcoming
To all guests, even thieves.
But considering that they are going South and I am not,
I wish they would bathe more quietly,
It is unmannerly to flaunt one's good fortune.

They rate me of no consequence,
But they might reflect that it is my gutter.
I know their opinion of me,
Because one is drying himself on the window-sill
Not two feet from my hand.
His purple neck is sleek with water,
And the fellow preens his feathers for all the world as if I
    were a fountain statue.
If it were not for the window,
I am convinced he would light on my head.
Tyrian-feathered freebooter,
Appropriating my delightful gutter with so extravagant
    an ease,
You are as cool a pirate as ever scuttled a ship,
And are you not scuttling my Summer with every peck of
    your sharp bill?

But there is a cloud over the beech-tree,
A quenching cloud for lemon-livered suns.
The grackles are all swinging in the tree-tops,
And the wind is coming up, mind you.
That boom and reach is no Summer gale,
I know that wind,
It blows the Equinox over seeds and scatters them,
It rips petals from petals, and tears off half-turned leaves.
There is rain on the back of that wind.
Now I would keep the grackles,

I would plead with them not to leave me.
I grant their coming, but I would not have them go.
It is a milestone, this passing of grackles.
A day of them, and it is a year gone by.
There is magic in this and terror,
But I only stare stupidly out of the window.
The grackles have come.

Come! Yes, they surely came.
But they have gone.
A moment ago the oak was full of them,
They are not there now.
Not a speck of a black wing,
Not an eye-peep of a purple head.
The grackles have gone,
And I watch an Autumn storm
Stripping the garden,
Shouting black rain challenges
To an old, limp Summer
Laid down to die in the flower-beds.

7

Free Fantasia On Japanese Themes

All the afternoon there has been a chirping of birds,
And the sun lies warm and still on the western side of
swollen branches,
There is no wind;
Even the little twigs at the ends of branches do not move,
And the needles of the pines are solid
Bands of inarticulated blackness
Against the blue-white sky.
Still, but alert;
And my heart is still and alert,
Passive with sunshine
Avid of adventure.

I would experience new emotions,
Submit to strange enchantments,
Bend to influences
Bizarre, exotic,
Fresh with burgeoning.
I would climb a sacred mountain
Struggle with other pilgrims up a steep path through
pine trees,
Above to the smooth, treeless slopes,
And prostrate myself before a painted shrine,
Beating my hands upon the hot earth,
Quieting my eyes upon the distant sparkle
Of the faint spring sea.

I would recline upon a balcony
In purple curving folds of silk,
And my dress should be silvered with a pattern
Of butterflies and swallows,

And the black band of my *obi*
Should flash with gold circular threads,
And glitter when I moved.
I would lean against the railing
While you sang to me of wars
Past and to come—
Sang, and played the *samisen,*
Perhaps I would beat a little hand drum
In time to your singing;
Perhaps I would only watch the play of light
Upon the hilt of your two swords.

I would sit in a covered boat,
Rocking slowly to the narrow waves of a river,
While above us, an arc of moving lanterns,
Curved a bridge,
A hiss of gold
Blooming out of darkness,
Rockets exploded,
And died in a soft dripping of colored stars.
We would float between the high trestles,
And drift away from the other boats,
Until the rockets flared soundless,
And their falling stars hung silent in the sky,
Like wistaria clusters above the ancient entrance of a
temple.

I would anything
Rather than this cold paper;
With outside, the quiet sun on the sides of burgeoning
branches,
And inside, only my books.

Solitaire

When night drifts along the streets of the city,
And sifts down between the uneven roofs,
My mind begins to peek and peer.
It plays at ball in old, blue Chinese gardens,
And shakes wrought dice-cups in Pagan temples
Amid the broken flutings of white pillars.
It dances with purple and yellow crocuses in its hair,
And its feet shine as they flutter over drenched grasses.
How light and laughing my mind is,
When all good folk have put out their bedroom candles,
And the city is still!

Wind And Silver

Greatly shining,
The Autumn moon floats in the thin sky;
And the fish-ponds shake their backs and flash their
 dragon scales
As she passes over them.

Night Clouds

The white mares of the moon rush along the sky
Beating their golden hoofs upon the glass Heavens;
The white mares of the moon are all standing on their
hind legs
Pawing at the green porcelain doors of the remote Heavens.
Fly, mares!
Strain your utmost,
Scatter the milky dust of stars,
Or the tiger sun will leap upon you and destroy you
With one lick of his vermilion tongue.

Hippocrene

With you,
  I sup on singing birds
And drink hot sunlight cooled with clouds.

With you,
  I ride the slanting winds,
Toss colored balls back and forth over the moon,
Swing up through trees,
And slide down swiftly upon beds of irises.

When you are here,
  We stack words at the end of a rainbow
And bowl at them with swans' eggs.

We run races through grass
  to old bronze temples,
And sitting under marble porches,
Count daisy petals
  to the tapping of a bell.

We leap from steeples,
And land in flowered palaces.

In cedar-scented parlours you tell me tales,
Long, slow tales,
  strummed lightly on a lute;
And I lie on blue cushions and watch the sea
  and hear your voice.

With you,
   I do all these things—
How therefore should I care
   to gabble with the donkey-men,
To gossip with the old women
   who sell turkeys,
To watch my next-door neighbor plait her hair
   and lament the untoward price of butter.

Until you come I will sit here
   alone, by a quiet window,
And, with a fine brush,
   trace little pictures
To show when you return.

The Humming-Birds

Up—up—water shooting,
Jet of water, white and silver,
Tinkling with the morning sun-bells.
Red as sun-blood, whizz of fire,
Shock of fire-spray and water.
It is the humming-birds flying against the stream
of the fountain.
The trumpet-vine bursts into a scatter of humming-birds,
The scarlet-throated trumpet flowers explode with
humming-birds.
The fountain waits to toss them diamonds.
I clasp my hands over my heart
Which will not let loose its humming-birds,
Which will not break to green and ruby,
Which will not let its wings touch air.
Pound and hammer me with irons,
Crack me so that flame can enter,
Pull me open, loose the thunder
Of wings within me.
Leave me wrecked and consoled,
A maker of humming-birds
Who dare bathe in a leaping water.

Twenty-Four Hokku On A Modern Theme

1

Again the larkspur,
Heavenly blue in my garden.
They, at least, unchanged.

2

How have I hurt you?
You look at me with pale eyes,
But these are my tears.

3

Morning and evening—
Yet for us once long ago
Was no division.

4

I hear many words.
Set an hour when I may come
Or remain silent.

5

In the ghostly dawn
I write new words for your ears—
Even now you sleep.

6

This then is morning.
Have you no comfort for me
Cold-colored flowers?

7

My eyes are weary
Following you everywhere.
Short, oh short, the days!

8

When the flower falls
The leaf is no more cherished.
Every day I fear.

9

Even when you smile
Sorrow is behind your eyes.
Pity me, therefore.

10

Laugh—it is nothing.
To others you may seem gay,
I watch with grieved eyes.

11

Take it, this white rose.
Stems of roses do not bleed;
Your fingers are safe.

12

As a river-wind
Hurling clouds at a bright moon,
So am I to you.

13

Watching the iris,
The faint and fragile petals—
How am I worthy?

14

Down a red river
I drift in a broken skiff.
Are you then so brave?

15

Night lies beside me
Chaste and cold as a sharp sword.
It and I alone.

16

Last night it rained.
Now, in the desolate dawn,
Crying of blue jays.

17

Foolish so to grieve,
Autumn has its colored leaves—
But before they turn?

18

Afterwards I think:
Poppies bloom when it thunders.
Is this not enough?

19

Love is a game—yes?
I think it is a drowning:
Black willows and stars.

20

When the aster fades
The creeper flaunts in crimson.
Always another!

21

Turning from the page,
Blind with a night of labor,
I hear morning crows.

22

A cloud of lilies,
Or else you walk before me.
Who could see clearly?

23

Sweet smell of wet flowers
Over an evening garden.
Your portrait, perhaps?

24

Staying in my room,
I thought of the new Spring leaves.
That day was happy.

The Anniversary

Ten years is nothing,
Yet I do not remember
What happened before.

Morning flings shadows,
But midday is shadowless.
So I have found it.

I have no flowers,
Yet I give you these roses.
Humor my pretence.

Have I satisfied?
Who can be sure of himself.
Touch me with your love.

Knowing my weakness,
Spread your hands above my head.
See only your hands.

Watching you daily,
I dare not think what I see.
It is better so.

Since I am only
What you may consider me,
Have merciful thoughts.

Shield me from myself.
At times I have wounded you.
I do not forget.

Take what I give you.
Foolishness is in my words,
But not in my heart.

Cease urging your ears,
My speech has little for them.
Hearken otherwise.

You wrong me, saying:
One death will not kill us both.
Your veins hold my sap.

Keep in remembrance:
Peonies do not blossom
Till Spring is over.

You prefer Spring? Why?
A season's length of hours—
Incalculable.

Days and days—what then?
Is not recurrence a smile
On the face of age?

Now, in the pale dawn,
How strange to consider time.
What is it to us?

Grains of rice counted—
Can any one so spend life?
Be spacious and wise.

The bowl is still full.
We will not be niggardly.
Plunge in both your hands.

I have known terror.
I swear to know it no more.
Each day a new dawn.

Youth is incautious.
Wisdom learns to tread softly,
Valuing moments.

Cherishing what is,
The wise man sees it depart
Without emotion.

Time is rhetoric,
A mad logician's plaything.
O pitiful world!

Listen to the wind;
Man has not learnt to measure
The wind of his thought.

Blowing asunder,
Yet we shall be as the air
Still undivided.

Sleep until day-spring.
With morning we start again,
Another ten years.

Ombre Chinoise

Red foxgloves against a yellow wall streaked with
plum-colored shadows;
A lady with a blue and red sunshade;
The slow dash of waves upon a parapet.
That is all.
Non-existent—immortal—
As solid as the center of a ring of fine gold.

8

Eleonora Duse

1

Seeing's believing, so the ancient word
Chills buds to shrivelled powder flecks, turns flax
To smoky heaps of straw whose small flames wax
Only to gasp and die. The thing's absurd!
Have blind men ever seen or deaf men heard?
What one beholds but measures what one lacks.
Where is the prism to draw gold from blacks,
Or flash the iris colors of a bird?
Not in the eye, be sure, nor in the ear,
Nor in an instrument of twisted glass,
Yet there are sights I see and sounds I hear
Which ripple me like water as they pass.
This that I give you for a dear love's sake
Is curling noise of waves marching along a lake.

2

A letter or a poem—the words are set
To either tune. Be careful how you slice
The flap which is held down by this device
Impressed upon it. In one moment met
A cameo, intaglio, a fret
Of workmanship, and I. Like melted ice
I took the form and froze so, turned precise
And brittle seal, a creed in silhouette.
Seeing's believing? What then would you see?
A chamfered dragon? Three spear-heads of steel?
A motto done in flowered charactry?
The thin outline of Mercury's winged heel?
Look closer, do you see a name, a face,
Or just a cloud dropped down before a holy place?

3

Lady, to whose enchantment I took shape
So long ago, though carven to your grace,
Bearing, like quickened wood, your sweet sad face
Cut in my flesh, yet may I not escape
My limitations: words that jibe and gape
After your loveliness and make grimace
And travesty where they should interlace
The weave of sun-spun ocean round a cape.
Pictures then must contain you, this and more,
The sigh of wind floating on ripe June hay,
The desolate pulse of snow beyond a door,
The grief of mornings seen as yesterday.
All that you are mingles as one sole cry
To point a world aright which is so much awry.

4

If Beauty set her image on a stage
And bid it mirror moments so intense
With passion and swift largess of the sense
To a divine exactness, stamp a page
With mottoes of hot blood, and disengage
No atom of mankind's experience,
But lay the soul's complete incontinence
Bare while it tills grief's gusty acreage.
Doing this, you, spon-image to her needs,
She picked to pierce, reveal, and soothe again,
Shattering by means of you the tinsel creeds
Offered as meat to the pinched hearts of men.
So, sacrificing you, she fed those others
Who bless you in their prayers even before their mothers.

5

Life seized you with her iron hands and shook
The fire of your boundless burning out
To fall on us, poor little ragged rout
Of common men, till like a flaming book
We, letters of a message, flashed and took
The fiery flare of prophecy, devout
Torches to bear your oil, a dazzling shout,
The liquid golden running of a brook.
Who, being upborne on racing streams of light,
Seeing new heavens sprung from dusty hells,
Considered you, and what might be your plight,
Robbed, plundered—since Life's cruel plan compels
The perfect sacrifice of one great soul
To make a myriad others even a whit more whole.

6

Seeing you stand once more before my eyes
In your pale dignity and tenderness,
Wearing your frailty like a misty dress
Draped over the great glamour which denies
To years their domination, all disguise
Time can achieve is but to add a stress,
A finer fineness, as though some caress
Touched you a moment to a strange surprise.
Seeing you after these long lengths of years,
I only know the glory come again,
A majesty bewildered by my tears,
A golden sun spangling slant shafts of rain,
Moonlight delaying by a sick man's bed,
A rush of daffodils where wastes of dried leaves spread.

Nuit Blanche

I want no horns to rouse me up tonight,
And trumpets make too clamorous a ring
To fit my mood, it is so weary white
I have no wish for doing any thing.

A music coaxed from humming strings would please;
Not plucked, but drawn in creeping cadences
Across a sunset wall where some Marquise
Picks a pale rose amid strange silences.

Ghostly and vaporous her gown sweeps by
The twilight dusking wall, I hear her feet
Delaying on the gravel, and a sigh,
Briefly permitted, touches the air like sleet.

And it is dark, I hear her feet no more.
A red moon leers beyond the lily-tank.
A drunken moon ogling a sycamore,
Running long fingers down its shining flank.

A lurching moon, as nimble as a clown,
Cuddling the flowers and trees which burn like glass
Red, kissing lips, I feel you on my gown—
Kiss me, red lips, and then pass—pass.

Music, you are pitiless tonight.
And I so old, so cold, so languorously white.